The Wisdom of Merlin

7 MAGICAL WORDS
FOR A
MEANINGFUL LIFE

T. A. BARRON

PHILOMEL BOOKS
AN IMPRINT OF PENGUIN GROUP (USA)

To the wizard who inspired the words

PHILOMEL BOOKS

Published by the Penguin Group | Penguin Group (USA) LLC
375 Hudson Street, New York, NY 10014
USA | Canada | UK | Ireland | Australia |New Zealand | India | South Africa | China
penguin.com | A Penguin Random House Company

Library of Congress Cataloging-in-Publication Data
Barron, T. A. The wisdom of Merlin : 7 magical words for a meaningful life / T. A. Barron.
pages cm   Summary: "A fictional guide to life and values, as told from the imagined perspective of Merlin, for graduates and others"—Provided by publisher.
1. Barron, T. A.—Philosophy. 2. Merlin (Legendary character) 3. Conduct of life. 4. Gift books. I. Title. PS3552.A737W57 2015 814'.54—dc23 2014015977
Printed in the United States of America.
ISBN 978-0-399-17325-7
1 3 5 7 9 10 8 6 4 2
Edited by Jill Santopolo. | Design by Semadar Megged.
Text set in 13/19-point Perpetua Std.

Contents

Merlin's
7 Most Magical
Words

Welcome to my Crystal Cave.

I do love visitors! Just as I love to explore the world outside my cave, visiting others near and far, as I've done for many centuries. (Don't get me started on how much I enjoy today's ice cream parlors and bakeries.)

Shall we talk about whatever questions you might have? Perhaps something small and simple. Like . . .

What is the meaning of life?

And . . .

How can I possibly find it?

Well, the answer to both those questions is surprisingly brief. It's the same answer—and it has *only seven words.*

That's right. Only seven. And they are *the most magical words* in the universe.

Now, my friend, follow me and I'll explain.

4

Gratitude

*H*olding his staff, Merlin walks into his cave. Whenever he passes near the sparkling crystals, they grow brighter, shift colors, or do something even more surprising. A deep purple amethyst releases an aroma of lilacs; an especially large ruby makes the sound of a gong that echoes around the cave.

Finally, he reaches an ancient, gnarled oak tree that looks even older than the wizard himself.

Every leaf on every branch shimmers with magic.
As Merlin approaches, the tree twists into a seat,
opening its branches to welcome him.

    Merlin sits down, breathes a grateful sigh, and
speaks.

GRATITUDE is first among the magical words, for it is a good place to begin to make a meaningful life. To be wholly alive is to be grateful—for every breath we take, every song we sing, every person we love, every day we discover.

Just being grateful helps us to notice and appreciate all the blessings and opportunities around us. Some people like to start their day

with a bowlful of cereal—but for me, it's a bowlful of gratitude!

All we have—truly all we have—is our time and our souls. Even if you live as long as a wizard, that time is really very brief. It's never long enough to do all you can do and be all you can be.

My friend Methuselah (an old friend in every way) once told me that the only time we have is now. So let's be grateful for that time—and live it well.

Each day, take a moment just to be. To love a person, a place, or an idea that has touched

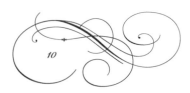

your heart. Cherish those blessings through all the seasons of a year—and all the seasons of your life.

Now . . . a truly radical thought: Sometimes, turn off your electronic equipment—all of it. Why do such a rash thing? Because being serene and quiet now and then gives us the space to feel grateful. You see, being *fully scheduled* is not the same as being *fully alive*. As I heard in Saint Paul's Church a few centuries ago, in a poem called "Desiderata": *Go placidly amid the noise and haste, and remember what peace there may be in silence.*

My favorite place to feel grateful is in nature—under a starry sky in the Scottish Highlands, by the vast ocean at the Great Barrier Reef, or in a grove of towering redwoods in California. Or, let me add, in a meadow of wild heather right here outside my home.

Here's the miracle of such places: With nature's wonders all around, I feel both very small and very large *at once*—diminished and humbled by my own insignificance, while *also* enlarged and inspired by the vast sweep of creation. And both you and I belong to that creation! For we are all made from miracles, no less than the stars themselves.

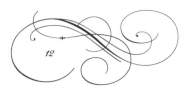

One of humanity's great challenges is to embrace nature without suffocating it—to treat our natural home with appreciation, not exploitation. We have been given the garden planet of the universe—and we can either nurture or devour it, protect or destroy it.

Fortunately, we have one great advantage in facing any challenges: ourselves. We can accomplish *anything* if we truly devote ourselves to the task.

And that, my friend, is worthy of our gratitude.

Courage

*A*n owl hoots from somewhere in the shadows, then glides over to land on Merlin's hand. The little fellow sighs longingly and twists his round face toward the cave entrance. He seems to be asking Merlin whether or not to leave—to venture outside the Crystal Cave.

The old wizard lifts the owl closer and peers into the bird's wide golden eyes. Quietly, he says, "If you stay here, you will never find her again.

*That's certain. Yet if you take the risk and go . . .
you just might."*

*With another hoot and a rustle of wings, the
owl takes flight. He floats away, leaving only the
fading echo of his voice.*

*Merlin watches him depart and whispers,
"Courage, my friend."*

COURAGE is essential. How else can we dream of who we can become and what we want for the world? And it also takes courage to turn those dreams into reality.

You see, life can have great meaning—but only if we discover that meaning for ourselves. Meaning can't be bought at any store. And it can't be handed down like a coat that someone tells you will fit perfectly before you've even

tried it on. Meaning must be sought and earned and made one's own.

All of which requires courage.

Have you ever stopped to wonder why we have free will to make our own choices—some wise and gracious, some just plain foolish, some catastrophically bad? Because our choices *matter*. They define who we are, what values we live by, and what aspirations we honor. And if our choices matter . . . then *we ourselves matter*.

Think of your life as a story—a story of which *you* are the author. Using whatever materials you have and whatever inspiration you

find, make it a story that truly belongs to you. Tell it with honesty; tell it with passion. And make it the very best story you can!

Come to think of it . . . I gave that same advice a while ago to an aspiring young bard who dropped by for a visit, much as you have. A rather likable chap by the name of Will. I encouraged him to write a decent sonnet or two.

Now, as Will said to me, *Brevity is the soul of wit.* So let me sum all this up:

Be bold with your life! Live vigorously and gently, mindfully and sensuously. Explore whatever calls to you. Love fully and freely.

Run as fast as you can; walk as slow as you can. Taste it, touch it, tickle it!

Dream some big dreams, my friend. Then work hard to make those dreams come true. For if you don't, who will?

As you pursue your dreams . . . *persevere*. At the end of your days, what you'll most regret is not what you tried and failed—but what you never tried at all.

Take time to discover. Find harmony in cacophony, unity in diversity. When a mountain rises up before you—climb it. That's what that

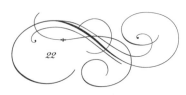

good chap Moses did, and look what *he* managed to find.

Above all, don't be just a consumer. Instead, be a *creator*. Of your own life, your own world, your own story.

Then go out and tell that story with courage.

23

knowledge

*S*uddenly crystals burst into flame!

　　That's how it seems, at least, as crystals on the walls, ceiling, and floor of the cave ignite with dazzling colors. They aren't really on fire, of course. But they're shining so bright, radiating purple and green and gold, they almost could be. All around Merlin, light fills the cave—a riot of radiance, a miracle to behold.

　　Then—a greater miracle. The colorful rays

combine, weaving together like luminous threads, making an awesome tapestry of light. It lasts just a few seconds, then starts to fade with the crystals' fire.

The wizard strokes his still-glowing beard. "I don't know how that happens," he muses. "But whenever it does, I feel centuries younger."

KNOWLEDGE, surprising as it sounds, begins with the unknown. With accepting how *little* you know. A few drops of humility, I've learned, can save me from an ocean of arrogance! Then, with a touch of curiosity . . . a person can learn and grow endlessly.

There are two universes to explore—one inside yourself and one outside. And here's the best part: How far you travel in each, and what you discover, is entirely up to you.

The first universe is yourself. Know who you are—honestly and deeply. Examine your passions, hopes, fears, strengths, weaknesses, and dreams. Seek only what is true, not what is comfortable.

Your vulnerabilities and your virtues are two halves of the same whole. Embrace the qualities in yourself that might seem like opposites—masculine and feminine, old and young, light and dark. Just as there can be no shadow without light, there can be no joy without sorrow.

Then, at last, you will know something of great value: *what you truly love.*

The second universe is everything outside yourself. Be alive in your world! Notice its many riches, struggles, delights, tragedies, patterns, revelations, and mysteries. Engage all your senses, all the time. Lengthen your attention span. Walk sensitively wherever you go.

Remember, as you explore, how much of the world you can see and hear and taste and smell and touch—and how much you cannot. Sometimes mindfulness means accepting the mystery of what lies beyond the reach of our minds.

And remember what I tried to teach young

Arthur when he began Camelot: A tool by it-self is not good or bad. Only how it's used de-termines that. A hammer can crush someone's skull—or build someone's home. The tool isn't as important as the purpose.

Then, at last, you will know something else of great value: *what the world truly needs.*

Now . . . connect those two great discover-ies: what you love and what the world needs. Combine them with care. And you are sure to live a marvelous life!

That, my friend, I know.

belief

*M*erlin turns in his chair, and the leafy branches move along with him. He points at a bare nub of rock on the cave wall—the only place with no crystals at all.

"Once in a great while," the wizard explains, "a crystal sprouts right there, blooming like a flower. And it's the most beautiful crystal in this whole cave. Just the sight of it makes my spirit soar! I'm never sure when it might appear or how

long it will last . . . but I look for it every day."

He sighs, peering at the bare rock. "There's no way to know if it will ever bloom again. But I believe it will."

BELIEF is a powerful elixir. It offers strength, renewal, and peace to those who drink it. And your cup can be forever refilled.

Follow your faith, as a river flows to the sea—and you will find yourself lapped by the gentle waves of the spiritual ocean that surrounds us all. To swim in that sea is to join with a greater power, a deeper awareness, a higher truth. And also . . . a quiet, enduring joy.

What inspires belief? The answer is different for each person. For me, it's the music of nature—the warm spring wind or the sound of a meadowlark. For Beethoven, it was the ringing hymn *Ode to Joy.* And for you . . . well, that's for you to discover!

To my mind, there's no need to debate about the description of heaven and hell. Those places are right here in our lives. Whatever else may lie beyond in the spirit realm, we create our own heaven and hell—by the choices we make in the lives we are given.

So I urge you to find your faith, believe in

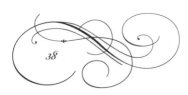

it, and act on its core values. That will bring heaven into your mortal life.

But take care with your faith, my friend. For it's all too easy to mistake belief for omniscience, to trade humility for arrogance. We are mortal beings, you and I—which means we are fallible. We make mistakes.

Which is why we cannot know with certainty the mind of God. Or absolute truth. We can only seek that mind, that truth, with honesty and devotion—and then trust in our beliefs.

So even in your chosen faith, remain tolerant of the faiths of others. As long as they don't

try to impose their ideas on you, or try to block your path to enlightenment, they have an equal right to explore whatever paths they choose. The wisest people in every faith understand and respect that.

Just remember: For your belief to be right, the beliefs of others need not be wrong! If you are truly secure in your own faith, truly touched by its wisdom and strength—then you don't need to convert anyone else.

Share your joy, if you like. But speak through actions more than words. That way, you will honor the searchings of others, even as you are buoyed by the waters of the spiritual sea.

And so . . . leave room for doubt. For doubt can be helpful, spurring us to look deeper and seek further. Your faith is only as strong as the questions you are brave enough to ask of it.

There will be times, alas, when belief may abandon you—when you cry out in pain, "Where is truth?" or "Where is God?" Certainly *not* with those who, in their arrogance, kill others in God's name. Or with those who try to dominate others through imposing a religion. Or with those who cut down virgin forests, despoil rivers and oceans, and destroy mountains—while assuring themselves they are doing God's will.

No, whenever I seek the peace and power of the greatest of spirits, I look in small, unremarkable places. In the eyes of a newborn child, and in the love of that child's mother. In a single snowflake that drifts down from the sky. In the glowing wings of a butterfly. In the surprising way a story can touch someone's heart.

In the unending power of all that and more, I do believe.

Wonder

*A*ll at once, something appears on that bare nub of rock near Merlin. It seems, at first, nothing more than a smudge of green, just a hint of reflected color from nearby crystals. Then . . . it starts to swell in size.

The wizard gasps. He watches, totally focused on what is sprouting from the stone.

A crystal! Rapidly, it expands, like a newly born flower pushing through the soil after a long

winter. Deep green, with touches of lavender blue, it rises out of the rock and opens petals that gleam more richly than emeralds.

"The flowering crystal," Merlin says in wonder. "It has returned, at last."

WONDER is the elemental wisdom of a child, a wisdom that is wide open to awe. For children see the world afresh, in all its beauty and strangeness, mystery and delight.

Too often, alas, adults lose their sense of wonder—just as I sometimes lose my bifocals or my staff. But I am glad to say they can all be found again.

You see, the wisest elder still has a child inside. A friend of mine is over a hundred

now . . . but she laughs and plays her piano with the delight of a seven-year-old girl. Indeed, my goal as a wizard has always been to grow younger with age!

To wonder is to open the doorway to imagination. And that leads to other doorways—appreciation, creativity, and fulfillment. That fellow Albert Einstein (someone I meet now and then on my journeys through space and time) knows a few things about theoretical physics. But what he knows *best* is how to imagine.

Who doesn't feel a rush of wonder when gazing up at the stars? And did you know that the same questions being asked today by astronomers

about the origins of the cosmos, the most enormous reaches of the universe, are also being asked by scientists who study subatomic particles, the most minuscule parts of the universe?

At the core of wonder is *openness*—being present, with all your senses alive. If you set out on a mission seeking wonder, you won't find it. Instead, take off your shoes, walk barefoot in the world . . . and allow it to happen.

Let life amaze you! Laugh freely; smell deeply; touch lovingly. Above all, feel the magic, the beauty, the surprise that surrounds you.

And then celebrate the wonder of it all.

Generosity

*T*he crystal flower starts to vibrate. At the same time, it releases a humming tone that grows steadily louder, echoing in the cave. Quickly, Merlin reaches over and cups his hands beneath the crystal—just as it breaks off from the wall.

The jeweled flower falls right into the wizard's hands, a newborn crystal held by those weathered old fingers. Each emerald petal glows radiantly, sending shafts of light all around. But nothing

glows brighter than Merlin's eyes as he gazes at the crystalline blossom.

"I will give this to a dear friend," he declares. "Of course, I'd love to keep it right here, where I can see it every day."

He grins. "Yet even more . . . I'd love to know it's with my friend, where she can do the same."

GENEROSITY is not giving others what they want. Rather, it's giving away what you yourself want.

Sharing requires empathy. So the physical act of making a gift is only part of what happens. It's the visible result of an earlier, *invisible* gift from the heart.

Besides, many of the best gifts aren't physical at all. Sure, give someone bread—or a lovely

crystal—whenever you choose. But also give freely of poetry, music, laughter, time, and hugs. As well as love and devotion, honesty and inspiration.

Think of the people whose generosity has touched your life—a parent, a teacher, a friend, or a kindhearted stranger. And then think of the generous spirits who have touched millions around the world. There are many of them. Even in just recent times, the list is long, including people like Jane Goodall, Nelson Mandela, the Dalai Lama, Helen Keller, Anne Frank, Isabel Allende, Mother Teresa, Mahatma Gandhi, and Martin Luther King, Jr.

Plant some generous seeds in the soil of your life. Yes—seeds that could grow into trees you may never see, in whose shade will gather people and creatures you may never meet. They will find joy and safety and solace under those boughs . . . and they will thank the person who made it possible.

Generosity multiplies. Whatever you give to someone inspires more gifts to others. And when you illuminate someone's path, many more will walk upon it. As my good friend Buddha would say, *Make of your life a light*.

Yes, indeed—a light that shines generously.

hope

*H*olding the crystal flower, Merlin gazes at its luminous facets. Tiny rivers of light seem to flow through every surface, pulsing gently, as if the crystal's emerald heart is beating in his hands.

The wizard shifts in his seat—and drops the crystal! It smashes on the cave floor, shattering into hundreds of shards.

Merlin cries out. He looks sorrowfully at the

floor. The light in every shard trembles for a few seconds, then goes out completely. Horrified, he watches the once-glowing pieces turn into lifeless rock.

"Will there ever be another?" he asks. "I can only hope."

HOPE requires courage. Especially in

our troubled world, with so much darkened by the shadow of despair, hope can seem elusive. Or even impossible.

Yet hope can return, on silent wings, when most needed. Whenever I would stop by to visit Emily Dickinson—she preferred not to leave her home, you see—she'd remind me how hope *perches in the soul.* How it's not the denial

63

of painful wounds, but the full awareness of those wounds—including the ways they could be healed.

That's why the essence of hope is transformation. Whenever I watch a caterpillar build a cocoon, sprout wings and fly—such an enormous change—it reminds me that I, too, can change. The mere existence of such a wondrous creature assures us all that, even in the darkness of our cocoons, metamorphosis is indeed possible.

Cynicism is the enemy of hope, always doubting that improvement (or even virtue) is possible. But fresh thinking is the ally of hope, reminding us of ways we can do better.

Alas, it's all too easy to be cynical—to constantly criticize people who try to help the world. To find imperfections is easy, especially from a safe distance. But to find solutions—that is difficult. Very difficult.

It takes valor to try, courage to engage. Let us celebrate honest efforts and high ideals! And, at the same time, let us always seek to improve.

We need heroes, people whose words and deeds inspire us to climb as high as we can on the mountainous trail of life. So . . . honor what good people have done. Then go out and find ways to do even better.

Blow on the embers of hope in yourself.

Strengthen them into flames. For those are the fires where new worlds are born.

Whenever I feel touched by despair, I think about two good sources of hope. They have revived my spirits many times over the centuries . . . and perhaps they'll do the same for you.

The first source is young people. Even if they sometimes don't realize it, young people have inner potential that glows brighter than any crystal! With their high ideals and wonder, their honesty and humor, they never fail to inspire me.

The second source is nature. With its awe-

some powers of resilience and renewal, nature has more magic than a million wizards! Even in the darkest days of winter, I remember that spring will come again.

Then, somehow, hope returns and settles in my soul.

And . . .

One More Word

*M*erlin stands and gazes around the Crystal Cave. "Now, my friend, you know the seven most magical words."

A mysterious gleam in his eyes, he adds, "There is, however, one more. It's the most magical word of all. And it's also the most varied—simple or complex, hidden or revealed, painful or joyous."

Merlin nods, his face alight. "That word is Love."

LOVE is an invitation, not a command. But if you truly open yourself to its power, you will be swept away as if you had plunged into a mighty river. Where that river may carry you, no one can predict.

One of my friends, who goes by the name Khalil Gibran, put it well: *A truly loving person doesn't feel that God is in his or her heart—but rather that he or she is in the heart of God.*

The paradox of love is that it beckons us to go deep *within* ourselves to find a soul-level understanding of another person. But once that understanding is found—we are bonded with that person so that we expand far *beyond* ourselves. We are, at once, deeper within and further without.

Love carries great peril, I must warn you. To open yourself to the power of love is to risk being hurt, perhaps deeply. Yet . . . to resist that power is akin to going through life with your eyes half closed and all your senses diminished. You may not suffer the greatest pains,

but you will also not savor the greatest delights. You won't feel agony, but you will also never experience ecstasy.

Love is a rope that can stretch itself infinitely. It can connect you to one person or many people. Its length can embrace a song, a book, a painting in oil or sand—any work of art. Its strength can link you forever to a place, a time, an experience, or an idea.

How do you express love? Through words and music and touch—really, through any kind of communication. The most powerful way, though, is simply how you *live*. And, as many

good people have shown the world, that power is truly limitless.

And now . . . here is a parting wish from your friend Merlin:

I wish you a life inspired by the seven most magical words—and by all the love that flows through them.